EMMANUEL JOSEPH

The Guardians, The ICC's Role in Modern Justice

Copyright © 2025 by Emmanuel Joseph

All rights reserved. No part of this publication may be reproduced, stored or transmitted in any form or by any means, electronic, mechanical, photocopying, recording, scanning, or otherwise without written permission from the publisher. It is illegal to copy this book, post it to a website, or distribute it by any other means without permission.

First edition

This book was professionally typeset on Reedsy.
Find out more at reedsy.com

Contents

1	Chapter 1	1
2	Chapter 1: The Birth of the ICC	3
3	Chapter 2: The First Cases	5
4	Chapter 3: The Challenge of Enforcement	7
5	Chapter 4: The African Backlash	9
6	Chapter 5: Expanding Horizons	11
7	Chapter 6: Gender Justice and the ICC	12
8	Chapter 7: The ICC and Non-Member States	14
9	Chapter 8: Environmental Crimes and the ICC	16
10	Chapter 9: The ICC and Global Diplomacy	18
11	Chapter 10: The ICC's Impact on National Justice Systems	19
12	Chapter 11: The Future of the ICC	20
13	Chapter 12: A Guardian for All	21

Chapter 1

Introduction

In an increasingly interconnected world, the need to understand and navigate the complexities of international law has never been more crucial. "Global Jurisdiction: Navigating International Law" offers an insightful exploration into the multifaceted world of international legal principles and their application. This comprehensive book delves into the foundational aspects of international law, including sovereignty, non-intervention, human rights, and the law of armed conflict, providing readers with a thorough understanding of these critical concepts.

The book begins by examining the historical development and sources of international law, setting the stage for a deeper exploration of contemporary issues. Readers will gain insights into the intricacies of human rights protection, the regulation of armed conflict, and the role of international courts and tribunals in enforcing legal norms. The chapters on international economic law and environmental law highlight the interplay between legal frameworks and global challenges, offering perspectives on trade, investment, and sustainable development.

"Global Jurisdiction" also addresses the evolving nature of international law in the face of emerging technologies, climate change, and shifting geopolitical dynamics. It underscores the importance of international cooperation and multilateralism in addressing transnational threats and fostering global peace and security. Through its comprehensive coverage and engaging narrative, this book serves as an indispensable resource for students, practitioners, and anyone interested in the dynamic field of international law.

Embark on a journey through the landscape of global jurisdiction and discover how international law shapes our world, resolves conflicts, and promotes justice and equity on a global scale.

2

Chapter 1: The Birth of the ICC

The International Criminal Court (ICC) was born out of a collective yearning for global justice. In the aftermath of the atrocities of World War II and the subsequent Nuremberg Trials, the world began to envision a permanent institution to hold individuals accountable for crimes against humanity. The Rome Statute, adopted in 1998, marked the formal establishment of the ICC, a court designed to transcend national boundaries and deliver justice where domestic systems failed.

The ICC's creation was not without controversy. Many nations, including powerful ones like the United States, China, and Russia, hesitated to join, fearing the erosion of their sovereignty. Yet, for smaller nations and victims of oppression, the ICC represented hope—a promise that even the most powerful could be held accountable. The court's mandate was clear: to prosecute genocide, war crimes, crimes against humanity, and the crime of aggression.

From its inception, the ICC faced immense challenges. Its jurisdiction was limited to crimes committed after July 1, 2002, and it could only intervene when national courts were unwilling or unable to act. Critics argued that the court was too slow, too bureaucratic, and too dependent on the cooperation of states. Yet, its supporters saw it as a necessary step toward a more just world.

The early years of the ICC were marked by cautious optimism. Its first cases focused on conflicts in Africa, drawing both praise and criticism. Some hailed it as a beacon of justice, while others accused it of bias. Despite these growing pains, the ICC began to carve out its place in the international legal landscape.

As the court took its first steps, it became clear that the ICC was more than just a legal institution—it was a symbol. It represented the idea that no one, no matter how powerful, was above the law. This principle would guide its journey through the complexities of modern justice.

3

Chapter 2: The First Cases

The ICC's first cases were a litmus test for its effectiveness and credibility. In 2004, the court opened its inaugural investigation into the conflict in Uganda, where the Lord's Resistance Army (LRA) had terrorized civilians for decades. The case against LRA leader Joseph Kony and his commanders was a landmark moment, signaling the ICC's commitment to addressing even the most entrenched conflicts.

However, the Uganda case also exposed the court's limitations. Kony remained at large, evading capture and mocking the ICC's authority. Critics pointed to this as evidence of the court's impotence, while supporters argued that the mere issuance of arrest warrants sent a powerful message to perpetrators worldwide.

The ICC's next major case involved the Democratic Republic of Congo (DRC), where warlord Thomas Lubanga was charged with recruiting child soldiers. His trial, which began in 2009, was a historic moment—the first time the ICC had brought a defendant to trial. Lubanga's conviction in 2012 was a victory for the court, but it also highlighted the painstakingly slow pace of international justice.

These early cases underscored the ICC's dual role as both a legal body and a moral authority. While its practical impact was often limited, its symbolic significance was immense. For victims of atrocities, the ICC was a platform to have their voices heard and their suffering acknowledged.

Yet, the court's focus on Africa sparked accusations of bias. African leaders argued that the ICC was disproportionately targeting their continent while ignoring crimes elsewhere. This criticism would haunt the court for years to come, shaping its approach to future cases.

4

Chapter 3: The Challenge of Enforcement

One of the ICC's greatest challenges has been enforcing its rulings. Unlike national courts, the ICC lacks its own police force or military. It relies entirely on the cooperation of states to arrest suspects and enforce sentences. This dependence has often left the court powerless in the face of defiance.

The case of Sudanese President Omar al-Bashir exemplified this struggle. In 2009, the ICC issued an arrest warrant for al-Bashir on charges of genocide and crimes against humanity in Darfur. Yet, al-Bashir remained in power for years, traveling freely to countries that refused to arrest him. This blatant disregard for the ICC's authority exposed the limits of international law.

Enforcement challenges have also arisen in cases where powerful nations shield suspects from prosecution. For example, the ICC's investigation into alleged war crimes in Afghanistan faced significant pushback from the United States, which imposed sanctions on court officials. This confrontation highlighted the tension between global justice and national interests.

Despite these obstacles, the ICC has persisted. It has worked to build alliances with like-minded states and international organizations, strengthening its ability to enforce its mandates. The court has also sought to enhance its legitimacy by improving transparency and engaging more closely with affected communities.

The enforcement dilemma remains a central issue for the ICC. As the court continues to grapple with this challenge, it must balance idealism with pragmatism, striving to deliver justice in a world where power often trumps principle.

5

Chapter 4: The African Backlash

The ICC's relationship with Africa has been fraught with tension. While many African nations initially supported the court, this enthusiasm waned as the ICC focused heavily on African cases. Critics accused the court of being a tool of Western imperialism, targeting African leaders while ignoring crimes in other parts of the world.

This backlash reached a crescendo in 2016, when South Africa, Burundi, and Gambia announced their intention to withdraw from the Rome Statute. Although Gambia and South Africa later reversed their decisions, the withdrawals sent a clear message: the ICC's credibility was under threat.

African leaders argued that the court's focus on their continent undermined its legitimacy. They pointed to conflicts in the Middle East, Asia, and elsewhere, where similar atrocities were allegedly ignored. This perception of bias fueled calls for reform and greater African representation within the ICC.

The court responded by seeking to diversify its caseload and engage more deeply with African stakeholders. It opened investigations outside Africa, including in Georgia and Afghanistan, and worked to address concerns about fairness and impartiality.

The African backlash was a turning point for the ICC. It forced the court to confront its shortcomings and rethink its approach to justice. While the relationship remains complex, it has also spurred important conversations about the role of international law in a divided world.

6

Chapter 5: Expanding Horizons

As the ICC matured, it began to expand its focus beyond Africa. In 2016, the court opened an investigation into the conflict in Georgia, marking its first formal probe outside the African continent. This move was seen as a response to criticism of regional bias and a step toward a more balanced approach to justice.

The Georgia investigation focused on alleged war crimes committed during the 2008 Russo-Georgian War. It was a politically sensitive case, involving powerful nations with vested interests in the region. The ICC's decision to pursue it demonstrated its willingness to tackle complex and contentious issues.

Around the same time, the ICC launched a preliminary examination into alleged crimes in the Philippines under President Rodrigo Duterte's war on drugs. This marked the court's first foray into Asia, further diversifying its geographic scope.

These expansions were not without challenges. The ICC faced resistance from powerful states and skepticism from local populations. Yet, they also signaled the court's growing ambition and adaptability.

By broadening its horizons, the ICC sought to reaffirm its role as a global guardian of justice. It aimed to prove that no region, no matter how powerful or remote, was beyond the reach of international law.

7

Chapter 6: Gender Justice and the ICC

The ICC has been a pioneer in addressing gender-based crimes, recognizing that women and girls often bear the brunt of conflict and oppression. The Rome Statute explicitly includes sexual violence as a crime against humanity and a war crime, marking a significant step forward in international law.

One of the court's landmark cases in this area was the prosecution of Jean-Pierre Bemba, a Congolese warlord convicted of rape as a war crime in 2016. This case set a precedent, demonstrating that sexual violence could no longer be dismissed as an inevitable byproduct of war. It also highlighted the ICC's commitment to giving a voice to survivors, many of whom had long been silenced.

However, the ICC's efforts in this area have not been without challenges. Prosecuting gender-based crimes requires sensitivity and expertise, and the court has sometimes struggled to provide adequate support for survivors. Critics have also pointed out that the ICC's focus on high-profile cases often overlooks the systemic nature of gender-based violence.

Despite these hurdles, the ICC has made significant strides in advancing gender justice. It has appointed specialized advisors, developed guidelines for investigating sexual violence, and worked to ensure that survivors are treated with dignity and respect.

The court's work in this area underscores its broader mission: to deliver justice not just for states, but for individuals. By addressing gender-based crimes, the ICC has reaffirmed its role as a guardian of the most vulnerable.

8

Chapter 7: The ICC and Non-Member States

The ICC's relationship with non-member states has been one of its most contentious issues. Powerful nations like the United States, Russia, and China have refused to join the court, citing concerns about sovereignty and political bias. This has created significant challenges for the ICC, particularly when investigating crimes in these countries.

The United States' opposition has been particularly vocal. In 2002, the U.S. passed the American Service-Members' Protection Act, which authorized military action to free any American detained by the ICC. This so-called "Hague Invasion Act" underscored the deep mistrust between the U.S. and the court.

Despite this hostility, the ICC has sought to engage with non-member states. It has opened preliminary examinations in countries like Afghanistan and Palestine, signaling its willingness to pursue justice even in the face of resistance. These investigations have often been met with fierce backlash, but they have also demonstrated the court's independence and resolve.

The ICC's ability to navigate this complex landscape will be crucial to its future. By building bridges with non-member states and addressing their concerns, the court can strengthen its legitimacy and expand its reach.

The relationship between the ICC and non-member states is a reminder

CHAPTER 7: THE ICC AND NON-MEMBER STATES

that justice is not just a legal issue, but a political one. It requires diplomacy, compromise, and a steadfast commitment to the principles of fairness and impartiality.

9

Chapter 8: Environmental Crimes and the ICC

In recent years, the ICC has begun to explore its role in addressing environmental crimes. While the Rome Statute does not explicitly include environmental destruction as a crime, the court has recognized that such acts can constitute crimes against humanity or war crimes under certain circumstances.

This shift reflects growing global awareness of the link between environmental degradation and human suffering. From illegal logging to the poisoning of water supplies, environmental crimes often have devastating consequences for communities, particularly in developing countries.

The ICC's potential to prosecute these crimes was highlighted in 2016, when then-Prosecutor Fatou Bensouda announced that the court would prioritize cases involving environmental destruction. This decision was hailed by environmental activists, who saw it as a powerful tool for holding corporations and governments accountable.

However, prosecuting environmental crimes presents unique challenges. These cases often involve complex scientific evidence and require cooperation from multiple jurisdictions. The ICC will need to develop new expertise and strategies to effectively address this emerging area of international law.

The court's interest in environmental crimes marks an important evolution

CHAPTER 8: ENVIRONMENTAL CRIMES AND THE ICC

in its mandate. By expanding its focus to include these issues, the ICC is positioning itself as a guardian not just of people, but of the planet.

10

Chapter 9: The ICC and Global Diplomacy

The ICC's work is deeply intertwined with global diplomacy. Its investigations often have far-reaching political implications, influencing relationships between states and shaping international discourse on justice and accountability.

One example of this dynamic is the ICC's investigation into alleged crimes in Palestine. The case has sparked intense debate, with some countries supporting the investigation as a step toward justice for Palestinians, while others view it as an overreach that could undermine peace efforts.

The court's role in global diplomacy is further complicated by the fact that many of its cases involve sitting heads of state or high-ranking officials. Prosecuting these individuals can strain diplomatic relations and provoke retaliation, as seen in the case of Omar al-Bashir.

Despite these challenges, the ICC has sought to navigate the political landscape with care. It has worked to build alliances with like-minded states, engage with international organizations, and maintain its independence in the face of pressure.

The ICC's impact on global diplomacy underscores the interconnectedness of justice and politics. As the court continues to pursue its mandate, it must balance its legal responsibilities with the realities of international relations.

11

Chapter 10: The ICC's Impact on National Justice Systems

One of the ICC's lesser-known roles is its influence on national justice systems. By setting international standards for accountability, the court has inspired reforms in countries around the world, encouraging them to strengthen their own legal frameworks.

This "complementarity principle," which holds that the ICC should only intervene when national courts are unable or unwilling to act, has been a driving force behind this trend. Faced with the prospect of ICC intervention, many countries have taken steps to improve their capacity to prosecute serious crimes.

For example, the ICC's involvement in Colombia's peace process has spurred efforts to address crimes committed during the country's decades-long conflict. Similarly, the court's work in Kenya has prompted reforms aimed at combating impunity and strengthening the rule of law.

While the ICC's impact on national justice systems is often indirect, it is no less significant. By encouraging domestic accountability, the court is helping to build a more just and resilient world.

This aspect of the ICC's work highlights the importance of collaboration in the pursuit of justice. By working with, rather than against, national systems, the court can amplify its impact and foster lasting change.

12

Chapter 11: The Future of the ICC

As the ICC looks to the future, it faces both opportunities and challenges. The court has made significant progress in its first two decades, but much work remains to be done.

One key priority is addressing the perception of bias. By diversifying its caseload and engaging more deeply with underrepresented regions, the ICC can strengthen its legitimacy and broaden its appeal.

Another challenge is improving efficiency. The court has been criticized for its slow pace and high costs, which have undermined its effectiveness. Streamlining procedures and increasing transparency will be essential to building public trust.

The ICC must also adapt to emerging issues, such as cyber warfare and climate change, which pose new threats to global security. By expanding its mandate and developing new expertise, the court can remain relevant in a rapidly changing world.

Ultimately, the future of the ICC will depend on its ability to balance idealism with pragmatism. It must continue to champion the cause of justice while navigating the complexities of international politics.

13

Chapter 12: A Guardian for All

The ICC's journey has been one of triumphs and tribulations, of hope and heartbreak. It has faced criticism and resistance, but it has also inspired millions with its vision of a world where justice knows no borders.

At its core, the ICC is more than just a court—it is a symbol. It represents the idea that no one is above the law, that even the most powerful can be held accountable for their actions. This principle is as relevant today as it was when the court was founded.

As the ICC continues its work, it must remain true to its founding ideals while adapting to the challenges of a changing world. It must listen to its critics, learn from its mistakes, and strive to deliver justice for all.

The road ahead will not be easy, but the stakes could not be higher. In a world plagued by conflict and inequality, the ICC stands as a guardian of hope, a reminder that justice is possible, even in the darkest of times.

The story of the ICC is still being written. Its legacy will be shaped by the choices it makes today and the courage it shows in the face of adversity. As long as there are those who believe in the power of justice, the ICC will endure, a beacon of hope in an uncertain world.

Book Description for *The Guardians: The ICC's Role in Modern Justice*

In a world where power often overshadows justice, the International Criminal Court (ICC) stands as a beacon of hope. *The Guardians: The ICC's*

Role in Modern Justice is a compelling exploration of the court's journey from its ambitious beginnings to its current role as a global arbiter of accountability. This book delves into the triumphs, challenges, and controversies that have defined the ICC's mission to deliver justice for the most heinous crimes—genocide, war crimes, crimes against humanity, and aggression.

Through 12 meticulously crafted chapters, the book takes readers on a journey through the ICC's landmark cases, from prosecuting warlords in Africa to investigating crimes in Georgia and the Philippines. It examines the court's groundbreaking efforts to address gender-based violence, its struggles to enforce rulings in the face of political resistance, and its evolving role in tackling emerging issues like environmental crimes and cyber warfare.

But *The Guardians* is more than just a chronicle of legal battles. It is a deeply human story, highlighting the voices of survivors, the courage of prosecutors, and the resilience of communities torn apart by conflict. It also confronts the criticisms and challenges that have shadowed the ICC, from accusations of bias to the complexities of global diplomacy.

Written with clarity and insight, this book is both a tribute to the ICC's achievements and a call to action. It challenges readers to reflect on the importance of justice in an unequal world and to consider their own role in upholding the principles of fairness and accountability.

The Guardians: The ICC's Role in Modern Justice is a must-read for anyone interested in international law, human rights, or the ongoing struggle for a more just world. It is a story of hope, resilience, and the enduring belief that no one—no matter how powerful—is above the law.

www.ingramcontent.com/pod-product-compliance
Lightning Source LLC
LaVergne TN
LVHW021055100526
838202LV00083B/6241